FAST TRACK

FAST TRACK

ENGLISH FOR ADULT LEARNERS

BOOK 1A

Suzanne M. Griffin
Washington State Office of the Superintendent of Public Instruction

Patricia J. Brenner
University of Washington

D. Robert Callaway
ELS Language Center, Seattle, Washington

NEWBURY HOUSE PUBLISHERS
A division of HarperCollins*Publishers*

Director: Laurie E. Likoff
Development Editor: David Tillyer
Text and Cover Design: A Good Thing, Inc.
Cover Photo: © D.P. Hershkowitz/Bruce Coleman Inc.
Text Illustrations: Penny Carter, Marlies Merk Najaka, Norman Moore
Photos: Rachael S. Griffin
Printer and Binder: Malloy Lithographing, Inc.

Acknowledgments:

Jim Brown
Eric Bredenberg
Diane Cales
Rachel Hidaka
Seattle Central Community College
Basic Studies Division and Photography Department
ELS Language Center, Seattle
Michael, Rachael, Sarah, Christian, Daniel, and our parents

NEWBURY HOUSE PUBLISHERS
A division of HarperCollins*Publishers*

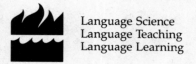

Language Science
Language Teaching
Language Learning

Fast Track: English for Adult Learners, Book 1A

Library of Congress Cataloging-in-Publication Data

Griffin, Suzanne M.
    Fast track : English for adult learners / Suzanne M. Griffin,
Patricia Brenner, D. Robert Callaway.
      p.   cm.
    ISBN: 0-06-632602-8 (bk. 1A)
    1. English language—Textbooks for foreign speakers.   I. Brenner,
Patricia J., 1945–   . II. Callaway, D. Robert, 1953–   .
III. Title.
PE1128.G679   1990
428.2′4—dc20
                                90-5637
                                CIP

                93 92 91   9 8 7 6 5 4 3 2

63–26029

We dedicate this book to adult second language learners.

CONTENTS

Unit 4

Unit 5

Unit 6

This series is about the Santos family and their first years in the United States. You will meet the relatives, co-workers, friends, and acquaintances who help them adjust to their new home in Seattle, Washington.

The material in this new ESL series for adults systematically introduces grammatical structures and language functions within the context of language competencies. Vocabulary, pronunciation items, and American cultural points are drawn from the two dialogs in each unit. Many life skills are covered that are not typically found in other programs.

Each unit in the student text has two lessons. Lesson 1 introduces an informal dialog and Lesson 2 introduces a formal dialog. Each lesson contains the following features:

The **Dialog** introduces the structures, functions, situations, and cultural focus of each lesson.

The **Comprehension** exercise orally checks students' understanding of the dialogs. Throughout the text, students are encouraged to expand their ways of indicating affirmation, confirmation, and negation in response to the statements or questions in this exercise.

The **Practice** exercise encourages students to use the dialog models to become familiar with American speech patterns. Gradually, they are guided in the incorporation of these patterns into their own speech. A summary of structures follows this exercise.

Match is an exercise which helps students recognize and match verbal and nonverbal behavior patterns.

Exchange, which is in the first lesson, exploits a variety of language functions and competencies found in the opening dialog of the unit.

Interact, which is in the second lesson, encourages students to apply structures, functions, or competencies from the lesson to their own experiences.

The **Apply** section at the end of each unit includes these features:

Express and Pronounce is an exercise which emphasizes stress, intonation, elisions, and sound discrimination patterns.

Notice Register encourages students to distinguish between formal and informal modes of expression and to understand the appropriateness of each.

Find Out About American Life presents life skill information and tasks to help students adjust to life in the United States. These tasks encourage students to explore further the ways to use their new language.

Show What You Know gives students practice in reading and completing authentic forms, schedules, and lists.

Test Your Knowledge reviews one or more of the focal points of the unit. Some exercises ask students to test their understanding of appropriate speech patterns. Others give them additional practice applying life skill information to real tasks.

Build Your Skills offers students opportunities to practice and extend the language and culture information introduced in the unit. They can do this section as homework or as independent work in the classroom.

FAST TRACK

LESSON I   At the Airport

🔊 LISTEN TO THE DIALOG

Roberto: Hey, Luis!
    Luis: Hello, Roberto! How are you?
Roberto: It's good to see you.
    Luis: It's good to see you. This is my wife, Maria.
          Is this Lydia?
    Lydia: Yes. It's nice to meet you, Luis and Maria.
   Maria: I am pleased to meet you.
    Luis: These are our children, Gloria and Ernesto.
Gloria and Ernesto: How do you do?
Roberto: Hi! Welcome to Seattle!

🔊 COMPREHEND

Listen to the dialog again.
Listen to the statements and respond.
Follow the model.

1. Roberto is at the airport.

2. Maria is at the house.

3. The children are at the airport.

4. Luis is at work.

5. They are at the airport.

6. They are in Los Angeles.

7. They are in Seattle.

8. It's 8:00.

9. It's 9:00.

10. Gloria and Ernesto are children.

Yes, that's right.

No, that's wrong.

Listen to the dialog. Check your responses.

PERFORM

Find partners.
Read the dialog aloud with your partners.
Close your books.
Try the dialog again.

PRACTICE

Exercise 1

Find a partner. Ask questions and respond. Follow the model.

Model: Maria **Partner 1: Is this** Maria? **Partner 2:** Yes, **this is** Maria.	**a.** Luis **b.** Ernesto **c.** Gloria **d.** Lydia **e.** Roberto **f.** _____

Roberto   Lydia   Maria   Luis

Ernesto   Gloria

Student   Teacher

Exercise 2

Find a partner. Ask questions and respond. Follow the model.

Model: wife **Partner 1: Is this** your wife? **Partner 2:** Yes, **this is** my wife, Maria.	**a.** son **b.** wife **c.** student **d.** husband **e.** daughter **f.** teacher

Husband   Wife

Son   Daughter

Teacher   Student

MATCH

Look at the pictures. Read the words. Match the words to the pictures.
The first one is done for you.

_____   ___1___   _____

1. It's good to see you.

2. This is my wife, Maria.

3. How do you do?

EXCHANGE

Find a partner. Introduce yourself. Follow the model.

Partner 1: Hi, I'm *Roberto*.
Partner 2: How do you do? I'm *Maria*.
Partner 1: It's nice to meet you.
Partner 2: It's nice to meet you, too.

Find a new partner. Introduce yourself. Follow the model.

Partner 1: Hi, I'm _____.
Partner 2: How do you do? I'm _____.
Partner 1: It's nice to meet you.
Partner 2: It's nice to meet you, too.

🔊 LISTEN TO THE DIALOG

Mr. Martin: Do you need a driver's license?
        Luis: No. I need an I.D. card. Here is my application.
Mr. Martin: Thank you. Are you Mr. Santos?
        Luis: Yes, I am.
Mr. Martin: Is this your present address? (Points to paper.)
        Luis: Yes, it is.
Mr. Martin: Is 285-7986 your telephone number?
        Luis: No, it's 285-1986.
Mr. Martin: O.K. Please stand here. I need to take your photo.

🔊 COMPREHEND

Listen to the dialog again.
Listen to the statements and respond.
Follow the model.

1. Luis is at the Department of Licensing.   **Yes, that's correct.**

2. Luis needs a driver's license.   **No, that's incorrect.**

3. Luis needs an I.D. card.

4. Luis has an application.

5. 285-7986 is his telephone number.

6. 285-1986 is his telephone number.

7. Mr. Martin needs to take Luis's photo.

Listen to the dialog. Check your responses.

PERFORM

Find partners.
Read the dialog aloud with your partners.
Close your books.
Try the dialog again.

PRACTICE

Exercise I

The information in this form is about Luis. Find a partner. Ask questions and respond. Follow the model.

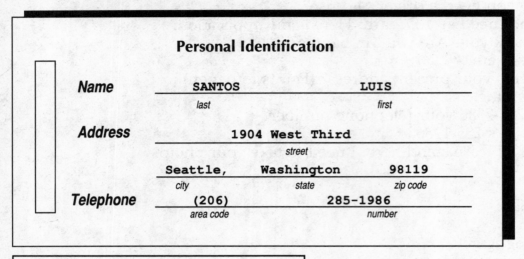

Personal Identification

Name	SANTOS	LUIS
	last	*first*

Address   1904 West Third
street

Seattle,   Washington   98119
city   *state*   *zip code*

Telephone   (206)   285-1986
area code   *number*

> **Model:** address
>
> **Partner 1: Is this** his address?
> **Partner 2:** Yes, **it is.**

a. name	**b.** street	**c.** state	**d.** area code
e. address	**f.** city	**g.** telephone	**h.** zip code

Exercise 2

Find a partner. Point to an illustration. Ask questions and respond. Follow the model.

Are you Luis?
Yes, I am.

Is he Luis?
Yes, he is.

Are you Gloria and Ernesto?
Yes, we are.

Are they Gloria and Ernesto?
Yes, they are.

Are you Lydia?
Yes, I am.

Is she Lydia?
Yes, she is.

Model: she _____

Partner 1: Is she Gloria?
Partner 2: Yes, **she is.**

---

a. he _____

b. she _____

c. you _____

d. they _____ and _____

e. you _____ and _____

f. _____ _____

SUMMARY

Is this his address?	**Yes, it is.**
Are you Luis?	**Yes, I am.**
Are you Gloria and Ernesto?	**Yes, we are.**
Is he Luis?	**Yes, he is.**
Is she Lydia?	**Yes, she is.**
Are they Gloria and Ernesto?	**Yes, they are.**

MATCH

Look at the pictures. Read the words. Match the words to the pictures.
The first one is done for you.

_____   __1__   _____   _____

1. Please stand here.
3. Here's my application.

2. No, it's 285-1986.
4. Is this your present address?

INTERACT

Find partners.
Look at the personal identification card.
Ask questions and respond.

Partner 1: Are you *Mr. Santos*?
Partner 2: Yes, I am.
Partner 1: Is this your *address*?
Partner 2: Yes, it is.
Partner 1: Is *285-9086* your telephone number?
Partner 2: No. My phone number is *285-1986*.

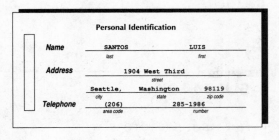

Now give your partner your identification card.
Ask questions and respond.

🔊 EXPRESS AND PRONOUNCE

Listen to these expressions.
Listen again and repeat.
Mark the expressions. Follow the model.

How do you do?   It's nice to meet you.

It's good to meet you.

Pleased to meet you.

How are you?   It's nice to see you.

It's good to see you.

Practice these expressions with another student.

NOTICE REGISTER

Make conversations with partners. Use a first name (Luis, Maria)
in the informal dialog. Use a title (Mr., Mrs.) in the formal dialog.

Informal

Partner 1: Hi, _____! It's good to see you!
Partner 2: It's good to see you! This is my friend, _____.
Partner 1: How do you do? Nice to meet you.
Partner 2: Nice to meet you, too.

Formal

Partner 1: Hello, _____! It's nice to see you!
Partner 2: It's nice to see you. I'd like you to meet _____.
Partner 1: How do you do? It's a pleasure to meet you.
Partner 2: It's nice to meet you.

FIND OUT ABOUT AMERICAN LIFE

I need an I.D. card. Here is my application.

Some people need an identification card (I.D.) in the United States.
You may need to show your age or your address.

Task

Go to the Department of Licensing or the Department of
Motor Vehicles. Complete an application. Take two information forms:
   1. Your birth certificate or passport
   2. A bill or rental agreement that shows your address.

SHOW WHAT YOU KNOW

Complete this form.

Personal Identification

Name		
	family	*first*
Address		
	street	
	city *state* *zip code*	
Telephone	( )	
	area code *number*	

TEST YOUR KNOWLEDGE

"How do you do?" and "How are you?" are not the same. Which is right?
The first one is done for you.

1. You meet a classmate for the first time. What do you say?

   How do you do? _____?

2. You see your teacher. What do you say?

   _____

3. You see a friend in the classroom. What do you say?

_____

4. You are with a friend. You meet his sister for the first time. What do you say?

_____

BUILD YOUR SKILLS

A. Complete. Use the words in the list.

Family Members	
husband	wife
son	daughter

Maria: This is Luis. He is my _husband_.

Gloria is my _____, and

Ernesto is my _____.

Luis: This is Maria. She is my _____.

My _____ is Ernesto, and my

_____ is Gloria.

B. Complete the words.

1. _H_ow are yo_u_?

2. This is my ___ife, Maria.

3. Is ___h___s Lydia?

4. Than___ ___ou.

5. Yes, ___t ___s.

6. It's ni___ ___ to meet you.

C. Read. Circle a or b. Write the response.

1. How do you do?
   It's nice to meet you.

   a. Thanks.
   (b.) It's nice to meet you.

2. Hey Luis!
   _____

   a. Hi, Roberto!
   b. How do you do?

3. Are you Mr. Santos?
   _____

   a. Yes, I am.
   b. Thank you.

D. Put these words in order.

1. is my This daughter   _This is my daughter_.

2. you pleased am I meet to   _____.

3. address present Is your this   _____?

E. Make questions. Respond with "yes."

1. she/Lydia
   Is she Lydia?   _Yes, she is._

2. they/students
   _____   Yes, _____

3. this/your address
   _____   Yes, _____

4. they/Luis' children
   _____   Yes, _____

5. you/a student
   _____   Yes, _____

6. this/your teacher
   _____   Yes, _____

7. this/Luis's photo
   _____   Yes, _____

F. Complete.

G. Complete Luis' driver's license.

NAME _____
              family   *first*

ADDRESS _____
                      street

_____
    city   *state*   *zip code*

H. Read the numbers:

0	1	2	3	4	5	6	7	8	9
zero	one	two	three	four	five	six	seven	eight	nine

I. Write the numbers:

1. Telephone Number
   two-zero-six   two-eight-four   six-seven-one-four

   (____ ____ ____)   ____ ____ ____ - ____ ____ ____ ____

2. Address
   one-four-seven N.E. Cedar Street, Apartment three

   ____ ____ ____ N.E. Cedar Street, Apartment ____
   Seattle, Washington nine - eight - one - nine - five

   Seattle, Washington ____ ____ ____ ____ ____

LESSON 1 In the Kitchen

🔈 LISTEN TO THE DIALOG

Lydia: Maria, what are you baking?
Maria: Apple pies.
Lydia: Mmm! Good! What's that?
Maria: Oh. I'm making bread now.
Lydia: You're a good baker, Maria.
Maria: Thank you.
Lydia: You know, our bakery is looking for a part-time baker.
Maria: Oh?
Lydia: Are you interested?
Maria: Yes.
Lydia: Can you come tomorrow?
Maria: Yes!

🔈 COMPREHEND

Listen to the dialog again.
Listen to the questions and respond.
Follow the model.

1. Is Maria baking?   **Yes, she is**.

2. Is Maria cooking?   **No, she isn't**.

3. Is Maria looking for a job?

4. Is the bakery looking for a part-time baker?

5. Is the bakery looking for a full-time baker?

6. Is Maria making bread?

7. Is Maria a good baker?

Listen to the dialog. Check your responses.

PERFORM

Find partners.
Read the dialog aloud with your partners.
Close your books.
Try the dialog again.

PRACTICE

Exercise 1

Find a partner. Ask questions and respond. Follow the model.

she / bake pies

> **Model:** she / bake pies
>
> **Partner 1: What is she doing?**
> **Partner 2: She's baking pies.**

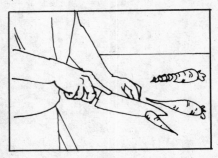

a. you / cut carrots

b. he / wash apples

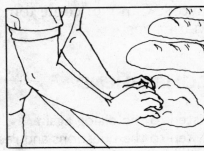

c. you / make bread

d. they / eat chicken

e. _____

SUMMARY

What are you doing?	**I am (I'm) baking** bread.
What is she doing?	**She is (she's) baking** bread.
What is he doing?	**He is (he's) baking** bread.
What are you doing?	**We are (we're) baking** bread.
What are they doing?	**They are (they're) baking** bread.

MATCH

Look at the pictures. Read the words. Match the words to the pictures.
The first one is done for you.

_____ _____ _1_ _____

1. What's that?

3. Oh?

2. Mmm! Good!

4. I'm making bread now.

EXCHANGE

Look at the pictures. Make four conversations with a partner.
Follow the models.

Partner 1: What are you doing?
Partner 2: I'm *baking apple pies*.
Partner 1: Oh. We're looking for a part-time *baker*. Are you interested?
Partner 2: Yes!

Partner 1: What are you doing?
Partner 2: I'm _____.
Partner 1: Oh. We're looking for a part-time _____. Are you interested?
Partner 2: Yes!

🔲 LISTEN TO THE DIALOG

Lydia: Maria, this is our head baker, Robert.
Maria: How do you do?
Robert: Pleased to meet you, Maria.
Maria: May I see the bakery?
Robert: Sure. We're baking rolls.
Maria: Oh. Are you making any bread today?
Robert: No. We aren't. We're making apple pies.

🔲 COMPREHEND

Listen to the dialog again.
Listen to the questions and respond.
Follow the model.

1. Is Robert the head baker?   **Yes, he is.**

2. Is Maria the head baker?   **No, she isn't.**

3. Is Maria at the bakery?

4. Are they making bread?

5. Are they baking rolls?

6. Are they baking apple pies?

Listen to the dialog. Check your responses.

PERFORM

Find partners.
Read the dialog aloud with your partners.
Close your books.
Try the dialog again.

PRACTICE

Read and Say

I am not	I'm not
you are not	you aren't
she is not	she isn't
he is not	he isn't
we are not	we aren't
they are not	they aren't

Exercise 1

Find a partner. Ask questions and respond. Follow the model.

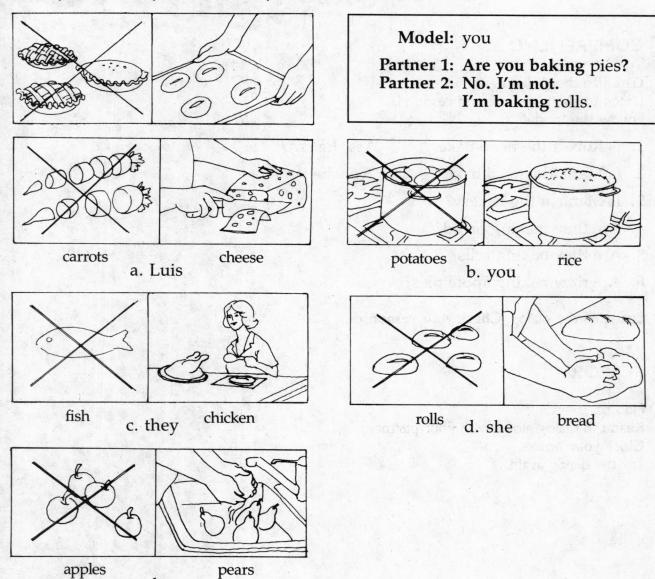

Model: you

Partner 1: Are you baking pies?
Partner 2: No. I'm not.
         I'm baking rolls.

carrots   cheese
a. Luis

potatoes   rice
b. you

fish   chicken
c. they

rolls   bread
d. she

apples   pears
e. he

SUMMARY

Are you baking pies?	No. I'm not. I **am baking** bread.
Is she baking pies?	No. She **isn't**. She **is baking** bread.
Is he baking pies?	No. He **isn't**. He's **baking** bread.
Are you baking pies?	No, we **aren't**. We **are baking** bread.
Are they baking pies?	No. They **aren't**. They're **baking** bread.

MATCH

Look at the pictures. Read the words. Match the words to the pictures.
The first one is done for you.

   1   _____   _____   _____

1. Pleased to meet you.   2. Sure.

3. No, we aren't.   4. May I see the bakery?

INTERACT

Find partners. Look at the pictures in **PRACTICE**, Exercise 1.
Demonstrate the action in one picture to your partners or to the class.
Follow the model.

        Student: Are you baking pies?
Demonstrator: No, I'm not.
        Student: Are you baking rolls?
Demonstrator: Yes, I am.

Now, a new student demonstrates an action.

🔊 EXPRESS AND PRONOUNCE

Listen to these expressions.
Listen again and repeat.

Formal	Informal
I am making bread.	I'm making bread.
You are a good baker.	You're a good baker.
She is a good baker.	She's a good baker.
We are baking rolls.	We're baking rolls.
I am not baking now.	I'm not baking now.
Robert is not baking bread.	Robert isn't baking bread.
They are not baking bread.	They aren't baking bread.

NOTICE REGISTER

Make three informal and three formal telephone conversations with partners. Follow the models.

Informal
Partner 1: Hello?
Partner 2: Hello. Is *Lydia* there?
Partner 1: *She's* busy. *She's painting the kitchen.*
Partner 2: Thanks. I'll call back. Goodbye.
Partner 1: Bye.

Lydia Santos	**Ernesto Santos**	**Maria Santos**
paint the kitchen	**eat dinner**	**plant flowers**

Formal
Partner 1: Hello?
Partner 2: Hello. May I speak to *Lydia Santos*, please?
Partner 1: I'm sorry. She isn't here. May I take a message?
Partner 2: No, thank you. I'll call back. Goodbye.
Partner 1: Goodbye.

FIND OUT ABOUT AMERICAN LIFE

You're a good baker.   Thank you.

Americans often compliment (say nice things about you). The correct answer is "thank you."

Task

Compliment your partner.

SHOW WHAT YOU KNOW

Read these numbers aloud.

0	2	5	8	13	14	16	19

Read these telephone numbers aloud.

(206) 323-9663   (415) 654-8840   (716) 447-1081

Read these zip codes aloud.

98007   10023   75075   94598   61821   01238

Say your telephone number.
Say your zip code.

TEST YOUR KNOWLEDGE

Match the jobs to the actions. The first one is done for you.

Gardener   baking bread
Baker   repairing cars
Mechanic   painting houses
Painter   planting flowers

BUILD YOUR SKILLS

A. Complete. Use the words in the list.

baking	I'm
call	please
goodbye	speak
hello	

Robert: Hello?

Maria: ___Hello___. May I _____ to Lydia, _____?

Robert: _____ sorry. She's busy. She's _____.

Maria: Thanks. I'll _____ back. Goodbye.

Robert: _____.

B. One word does not belong. Put an X on the word.

1. chicken   ~~help~~   eggs   bread
2. mechanic   gardener   flowers   baker
3. you   for   I   they
4. husband   daughter   wife   tomorrow
5. cook   make   good   bake
6. street   application state   city
7. washing   eating   bake   cutting

C. Find the correct word. Circle it.

Maria (is)/are in the bakery now. She is/are baking pies. Lydia and

Robert is/are working in the bakery, too. They is/are baking

bread. Lydia is/are baking bread and Robert is/are baking pies.

D. Look at the pictures. Write the questions.

1.

   what is she doing ?
   She's baking pies.

2.

   _____?
   No, she isn't.

3.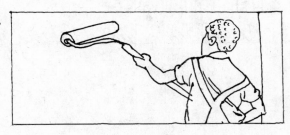

   _____?
   He's painting a house.

4.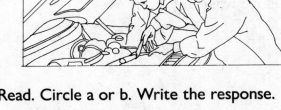

   _____?
   Yes, they are.

E. Read. Circle a or b. Write the response.

1. You're a good baker.
   Thank you.

   a. Thank you.
   b. Yes, I am.

2. What's that?
   _____

   a. It's bread.
   b. Of course.

3. May I see the bakery?
   _____

   a. Sure.
   b. No, we aren't.

4. Are you interested?
   _____

   a. No, thank you.
   b. It's nice to meet you, too.

F. Look at the pictures. Write the responses.

I am not	I'm not
(s)he is not	(s)he isn't
we are not	we aren't
they are not	they aren't

1.

Is she baking rolls?

No, she isn't. She's baking pies.

2.

Is he washing pears?

_____

3.

Are they eating fish?

_____

4.

Is Maria baking apples?

_____

5.

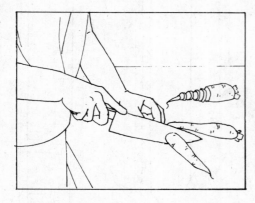

Are you cutting cheese?

_____

G. Read the numbers.

10	11	12	13	14
ten	eleven	twelve	thirteen	fourteen

15	16	17	18	19
fifteen	sixteen	seventeen	eighteen	nineteen

H. Look at the pictures. Write the number or the word.

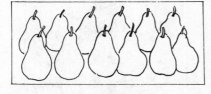      

__12__ _twelve_   ____ **fifteen**   __19__ _____

__10__ _____   ____ **fourteen**   ____ **eleven**

LESSON 1   In the Right Place

🔲 LISTEN TO THE DIALOG

Steve: Hi. Can I help you?
 Luis: I'm looking for a job.
Steve: A job? What kind of job?
 Luis: Mechanic.
Steve: You're in the right place.
 Luis: Good! Where is the office?
Steve: Go through that door and take the first right.
 Luis: Thank you.
Steve: Uh huh.

🔲 COMPREHEND

Listen to the dialog again.
Listen to the questions and respond.
Follow the model.

1. Is Luis at Nick's Auto Service?   **Yes, he is.**

2. Is Luis at the bakery?   **No, he isn't.**

3. Is he at Nick's Auto Service or at the bakery?   **He's at Nick's Auto Service.**

4. Is Luis looking for a job?

5. Is he looking for a cook's job?

6. Is he looking for a cook's job or a mechanic's job?

7. Is Luis in the right place?

8. Is Luis in the wrong place?

9. Is Luis in the right place or the wrong place?

Listen to the dialog. Check your responses.

PERFORM

Find partners.
Read the dialog aloud with your partners.
Close your books.
Try the dialog again.

PRACTICE

Read and Say

first (1st)   right (→)
second (2nd)   (←) left
third (3rd)

Exercise 1

Find a partner. Look at the map of rooms. Ask questions and respond.
Follow the model.

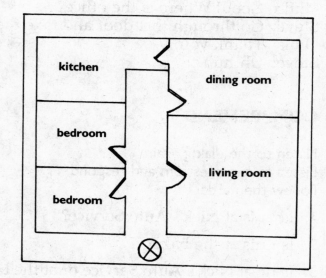

> **Model:** bathroom
>
> **Partner 1: Where is** the bathroom?
> **Partner 2: Go through the door.**
>   **Take the first left.**

a. living room   **b.** bedroom

c. bathroom   **d.** kitchen

e. dining room   **f.** _____

Exercise 2

Find a partner. Look at the map of buildings. Ask questions and respond.
Follow the model.

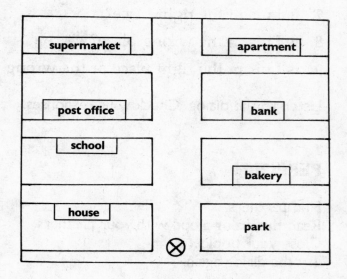

> **Model:** apartment
>
> **Partner 1: Where is** the apartment?
> **Partner 2: Go down the street.**
>   **Take the third right.**

a. bakery   **b.** school

c. post office   **d.** house

e. bank   **f.** supermarket

MATCH

Look at the pictures. Read the words. Match the words to the pictures.

_____   _____   _____   _____

1. You're in the right place.   **2.** Thank you.

3. Go through that door and turn right.   **4.** A job? What kind of job?

EXCHANGE

Look at the map. Make four conversations with a partner.
Follow the model.

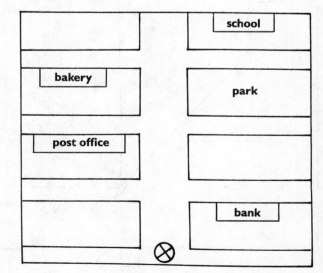

Partner 1: Hi. Can I help you?
Partner 2: Yes. Where is the *post office*, please?
Partner 1: Go *down the street*. Take the *second left*.
Partner 2: Thank you.

Partner 1: Hi. Can I help you?
Partner 2: Yes. Where is the _____ please?

Partner 1: Go _____. Take the _____.
Partner 2: Thank you.

TOM BUTLER

🔲 LISTEN TO THE DIALOG

Ann: May I help you?
Luis: Is there any work for me?
Ann: What kind of work are you looking for?
Luis: A mechanic's job.
Ann: Here's an application. Please fill it out.
Luis: All right. May I use this pen?
Ann: Yes. Oh! Don't fill out this part.
Luis: Okay. May I sit over there?
Ann: Yes. Take that chair.
Luis: Thank you.

🔲 COMPREHEND

Listen to the dialog again.
Listen to the questions and respond.

1. Is Luis in the office?

2. Is Luis at the airport?

3. Where is Luis?

4. Is Steve helping Luis?

5. Is Ann helping Luis?

6. What is Ann doing?

7. Is Luis filling out the application now?

8. What's Luis doing?

Listen to the dialog. Check your responses.

PERFORM

Find partners.
Read the dialog aloud with your partners.
Close your books.
Try the dialog again.

PRACTICE

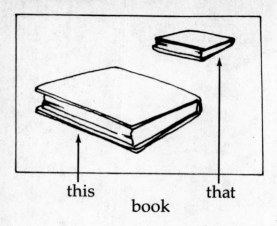

this   that

book

Exercise 1

Find a partner. Look at the pictures. Ask questions and respond. Follow the model.

chair

> **Model:** chair
>
> **Partner 1: Can I use this** chair?
> **Partner 2:** Yes, **you can**.
> **Partner 1:** Thank you.

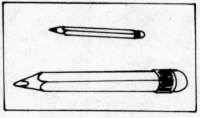

a. pencil

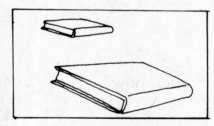

b. book

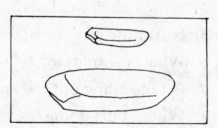

c. eraser

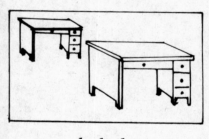

d. desk

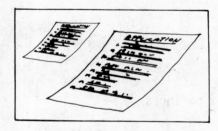

e. application

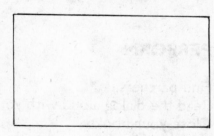

f. _____

Exercise 2

Find a partner. Look at the pictures. Ask questions and respond. Follow the model.

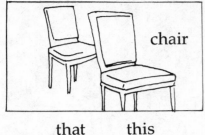

chair

that   this

Model: chair
Partner 1: **May I use that** chair?
Partner 2: **No.** Please **use this** one.
Partner 1: Okay.

SUMMARY

Can I use this chair?	**Yes, you can.**
May I use this chair?	**No, please use that one.**

MATCH

Look at the pictures. Read the words. Match the words to the pictures.

_____   _____   _____   _____

1. Here's an application.   2. May I help you?

3. May I sit in that chair?   4. A mechanic's job.

INTERACT

Where do you live? Where is your school? Take a walk around your school.
Make a class map with your teacher. Show the school, the bank, the park, the post office.
Now find partners. Ask and answer "where?"

Example:

Partner 1: Where is the school?
Partner 2: Go down the street. Take the first left.

📼 EXPRESS AND PRONOUNCE

In informal spoken English *can* sounds like [*kn*].
Listen to *can* in these questions.
Listen again and repeat.

> Can I help you?
> Can I use this pen?
> Can I sit over there?
> Can I fill it out?
> Can you come tomorrow?

NOTICE REGISTER

Make three informal and three formal conversations with partners.
Follow the models.

Informal
Partner 1: Hi. Can I help you?
Partner 2: Yes. *I'm looking for a job*.
Partner 1: A job? What kind?
Partner 2: *Mechanic*.

1. Mechanic   2. Painter   3. Gardener

Formal
Partner 1: Hello. May I help you?
Partner 2: Yes. *I'm looking for a job*.
Partner 1: What sort of position would you like?
Partner 2: *Mechanic*.

FIND OUT ABOUT AMERICAN LIFE

Is there any work for me?

This is not polite. This is better: "I'm looking for a job. Do you have any available?"

Task

Ask your partner for a job.

SHOW WHAT YOU KNOW

Complete this job application.

NICK'S AUTO SERVICE

_____   _____
Date   **Social Security Number**

NAME _____
           (LAST)   *(FIRST)*   *(MIDDLE)*

ADDRESS _____
                  (NUMBER & STREET)

_____
      (CITY)   *(STATE)*   *(ZIP CODE)*

TELEPHONE _____
         (AREA CODE)   *(TELEPHONE)*

Type of Work Wanted: *Full Time* ☐   *Part Time* ☐

TEST YOUR KNOWLEDGE

Make four *where* questions and four *what* questions. Answer the questions.
The first one is done for you.

Maria	in the bakery	bake rolls
Luis	in the office	fill out an application
Gloria	in the kitchen	make pies
the mechanic	in the repair shop	repair a car

1. _Where is Maria?_ _She's in the bakery._
   What is she doing? _She's baking rolls._

2. _____ _____
   _____ _____

3. _____ _____
   _____ _____

4. _____ _____
   _____ _____

BUILD YOUR SKILLS

Look at the map.

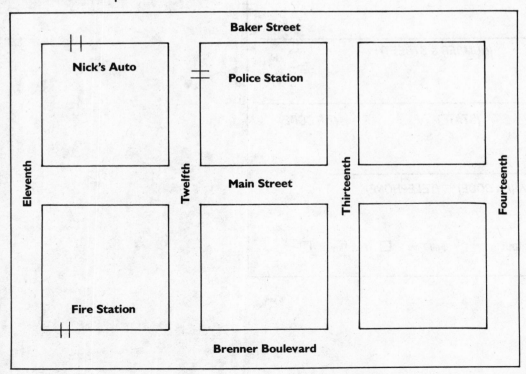

A. Complete.

AT THE BUS STOP

— Can I help you?

■ Yes, _where_ is the police station?

— Go _____ down _____ Street. Take the

_____ right. It's on the _____.

■ Thanks. Where _____ the fire department?

— _____ left down Main Street. _____ the first

_____. You're on Twelfth. Take the _____
right.

The fire station _____ on the right.

B. Read the response. Write the question.

1. _May I open that window?_
   No. Open this window.

2. _____
   Yes, you may sit in this blue chair.

3. _____
   No, Luis may not. He may use that eraser.

4. _____
   Yes, the children may sit over there.

5. _____
   Yes, Maria may use this car.

6. _____
   No, you may not. Use that chair.

C. Complete the crossword. Use the word list.

¹M				³		⁵
A						
²R						
I						
⁴A						

Word list:
```
are
bread
can
Maria
mechanic
not
```

Across

1. What is Luis' job?

2. What is Maria baking?

4. They ___ cooking now.

Down

1. Gloria's mother

3. She is ___ eating.

5. Hi. ___ I help you?

D. Read the numbers.

20	21	22	23	24
twenty	twenty-one	twenty-two	twenty-three	twenty-four

25	26	27	28	29
twenty-five	twenty-six	twenty-seven	twenty-eight	twenty-nine

Write the numbers for the problems:

1. Seventeen plus six equals twenty-three.

$$\begin{array}{r} 17 \\ +6 \\ \hline 23 \end{array}$$

2. Ten plus seventeen equals twenty-seven.

3. Twelve plus fourteen equals twenty-six.

4. Fifteen plus thirteen equals twenty-eight.

5. Eleven plus eighteen equals twenty-nine.

6. Sixteen plus five equals twenty-one.

7. Nineteen plus six equals twenty-one.

8. Eight plus twelve equals twenty.

9. Nine plus fourteen equals twenty-three.

10. Six plus sixteen equals twenty-two.

Look at the information.

MONTHS OF THE YEAR

January	1	May	5	September	9
February	2	June	6	October	10
March	3	July	7	November	11
April	4	August	8	December	12

Dates

Long Form				Short Form		
Month/	Day /	Year		Month/	Day /	Year
April	15	1989		4	15	1989

E. Complete.

1. November 12, 1985   *11/12/85*
2. May 2, 1942   _____
3. February 10, 1953   _____
4. _____   6/12/68
5. _____   10/29/85
6. _____   3/17/77

F. Complete.

	Long form	Short form
1. Today's date	_____	_____
2. Your birthday	_____	_____

UNIT 4

Luis: Hello. I'm Luis Santos. I . . .
Steve: I remember you! You're the new mechanic.
Luis: Yes.
Steve: I'm Steve Richmond. I work in the sales department.
Luis: It's nice to meet you, Steve.
Steve: Same here. Your supervisor is Tom Butler. He comes in at 9:00.
Luis: Oh. Do you have my tools?
Steve: No. Ask Bill Heming. He works at the service counter.
Luis: O.K. Thanks, Steve.

📼 **COMPREHEND**

Listen to the dialog again.
Listen to the questions and respond.
Follow the model.

1. Is Luis the new baker?   **No, he isn't.**

2. Is Luis the new mechanic?   **Yes, he is.**

3. Is Luis the new baker or the new mechanic?

4. Does Steve work in the bakery?

5. Does Steve work in the sales department?

6. Is Tom Butler Luis' supervisor?

7. Is Tom Butler a baker or a supervisor?

8. Does Tom come to work at 8:00?

9. Does Tom come to work at 9:00?

10. Does Tom come to work at 8:00 or 9:00?

11. What time does Tom come to work?

12. Is Bill Heming at the service counter?

Listen to the dialog. Check your responses.

PERFORM

Find partners.
Read the dialog aloud with your partners.
Close your books.
Try the dialog again.

PRACTICE

Exercise 1

Find a partner. Ask questions and respond. Follow the model.

Steve

> **Model:** Steve
>
> **Partner 1: Does Steve come** to work at 9:00?
> **Partner 2: Yes, he does.**

a. Maria

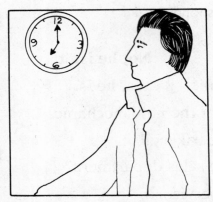

b. Luis

c. Bill

d. the gardener

e. the painter

f. the teacher

Unit 4 ■ LESSON 1

Exercise 2

Find a partner. Ask questions and respond. Follow the model.

> **Model:** Steve / in the sales department
>
> **Partner 1:** **Does Steve work** in the sales department?
> **Partner 2:** Yes, that's right. **He works there.**

Steve / in the Sales Department

a. Maria / in the bakery

b. Luis / at Nick's Auto Service

c. Bill / at Nick's Auto Service

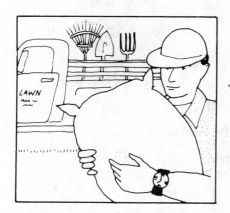

d. the gardener / at the nursery

e. the painter / at the house

f. the teacher / at school

SUMMARY

Does Tom come to work at 9:00?
Yes, he does.
Yes, he comes to work at 9:00.

Does Maria work in the bakery?
Yes, she does.
Yes, she works in the bakery.

MATCH

Look at the pictures. Read the words. Match the words to the pictures.

_____

_____

_____

_____

1. He works at the service counter.

2. I remember you!

3. Do you have my tools?

4. It's nice to meet you, Steve.

EXCHANGE

Find two partners. Introduce them. Follow the model.

Partner 1: _Luis_, this is _Bill Heming_. _He_ works at _the service counter_.
Partner 2: Hello, _Bill_. Nice to meet you.
Partner 3: Hi, _Luis_. Nice to meet you, too.

Now use your own names. Introduce your partners to each other.

🔊 LISTEN TO THE DIALOG

Tom: Welcome to our service department, Luis.

Luis: Thank you, Mr. Butler.

Tom: Here's your work schedule. You work from 7 to 4, Monday through Friday.

Luis: O.K. 7:00 to 4:00.

Tom: Be here on time. Customers usually bring in their cars early.

Luis: O.K. What time is lunch?

Tom: Go to lunch at 11:00. Be back at 12:00.

Luis: O.K.

Tom: Put your tools away at 4:00. Don't leave them out.

Luis: All right, Mr. Butler.

🔲 COMPREHEND

Listen to the dialog again.
Listen to the questions and respond.

1. Does Luis work from 8 to 5?

2. Does Luis work from 7 to 4?

3. Does he work from 8 to 5 or from 7 to 4?

4. Does Luis work Monday through Friday?

5. Does Luis work on Saturdays and Sundays?

6. Do customers bring in their cars early or late?

7. Is lunch from 11:00 to 12:00?

8. What time is lunch?

9. When does Luis put away his tools?

10. Does he leave his tools out?

Listen to the dialog. Check your responses.

PERFORM

Find partners.
Read the dialog aloud with your partners.
Close your books.
Try the dialog again.

PRACTICE

Verb List		
bring in	repair	eat
put away	wash	

Exercise 1

Find a partner. Use the verb list. Make sentences about each picture.
Follow the model.

you / I

<table>
<tr><td>Model: you / I</td></tr>
<tr><td>Partner 1: Do you put the tools away in the evening?
Partner 2: Yes, I do.</td></tr>
</table>

a. they / they

b. you / we

c. you / I

d. they / they

Exercise 2

Find a partner. Use the verb list and the pictures from Exercise 1. Ask
questions and respond. Follow the model.

you / I

<table>
<tr><td>Model: you / I</td></tr>
<tr><td>Partner 1: Do you put the tools away in the evening?
Partner 2: I put the tools away in the evening.</td></tr>
</table>

SUMMARY

Do you put the tools away in evening?
    Yes, I do. I put the tools away in the evening.
Do you put the tools away in evening?
    Yes, we do. We put the tools away in the evening.
Do they put the tools away in evening?
    Yes, they do. They put the tools away in the evening.

MATCH

Look at the pictures. Read the words. Match the words to the pictures.

_____ _____ _____ _____

1. Welcome to our service department, Luis.

2. Here's your work schedule.

3. Be here on time.

4. All right.

INTERACT

Find a partner. Ask questions.
Fill in the chart. Follow the model.

> **Model:** _breakfast_
>
> **Partner 1:** Do you eat _breakfast_?
> **Partner 2:** Yes, at _8:00_.

Use the chart.
Make a new dialog.
Perform for the class.

TIME	ACTIVITY
_8:00_	eat breakfast
	go to school
	study English
	eat lunch
	leave school

🔲 EXPRESS AND PRONOUNCE

Listen.
Listen again and repeat.
Mark the expressions. Follow the model.

Do you have my tools?

Does Steve work in the sales department?

Does he come to work at 9 o'clock?

Do customers bring in their cars early?

Are you Luis Santos?

Is lunch at 11 o'clock?

Is Luis the new mechanic?

Practice these questions with another student.

NOTICE REGISTER

Make conversations with partners. Use a first name (Luis, Steve) in the informal dialog. Use a full name (Mrs. Santos, David Martin) in the formal dialog. Follow the models.

Informal
Partner 1: Hi, I'm *Luis*.
Partner 2: Oh, I remember you, I'm *Steve*.
Partner 1: Glad to meet you.
Partner 2: Same here.

Formal
Partner 1: Hello. My name is *Lydia Santos*.
Partner 2: How do you do, *Mrs. Santos*. I'm pleased to meet you. My name is *David Martin*.
Partner 1: I'm pleased to meet you, too.

Now, use your name.

FIND OUT ABOUT AMERICAN LIFE

Luis: What time is lunch?
Tom: Go to lunch at 11:00. Be back at 12:00.

In the workplace, lunch break is usually 30 minutes or 60 minutes. It is usually between 11:00 and 12:00. Americans eat a small lunch.

Task

Ask three Americans these questions:

What time is your lunch break?
Is your lunch break 30 minutes or 60 minutes?

Then share the responses with the class.

SHOW WHAT YOU KNOW

Look at Luis Santos' work schedule.

Time	Activity
7:00	comes to work
7:30-9:30	repairs cars
9:30-9:45	takes a coffee break
9:45-11:00	repairs cars
12:00	eats lunch
4:00	puts tools away
4:15	leaves work

Now fill in your schedule.

Time	Activity

TEST YOUR KNOWLEDGE

Complete the sentences. Use the verb list. Follow the model.

> **Model:** Gloria _____comes_____ to school at 9:00.

1. Lydia _____ to the bakery at 9:30.

2. The baker _____ from 6:00 to 11:00.

3. Roberto and Lydia _____ to lunch at 12:00.

4. You and I _____ work at 5:00.

5. We _____ a coffee break at 9:45.

6. My wife _____ lunch at 12:30.

7. Bill and I _____ flowers in the morning.

8. He _____ cars in the morning.

9. Your teacher _____ away the books at 4:00.

10. The customers _____ in their cars in the morning.

Verb List
bring
come
eat
go
leave
plant
put
repair
take
work

BUILD YOUR SKILLS

Look at the schedule.

WORK SCHEDULE				
EMPLOYEE	*IN*	*OUT*	*IN*	*OUT*
TOM	9:00	12:00	1:00	5:00
LUIS	7:00	11:00	12:00	4:00
BILL	8:00	11:00	12:00	4:00
STEVE	8:30	12:00	1:00	4:30

A. Write the response.

1. When does Steve start work? _____

2. What time does Tom go to lunch? _____

3. Do Luis and Bill eat lunch at 11:00? _____

4. Do Luis and Bill return to work at 12:00? _____

5. When does Tom go to work? _____

6. Who leaves work at 4:30? _____

B. Put these words in order.

1. goes   at   to   Steve   Does   8:00   work?

_____

2. have   tools   you   my   Do?

_____

3. department   the   I   in   work   sales.

_____

4. to   like   don't   They   wait.

_____

5. you   meet   It's   Steve   to   nice.

C. Match

_____   _____   _____

1. Work ends at 4:00
2. How do you do?
3. What time is lunch?

D. Spelling: -ing

make	+ ing	⟶	making
bake	+ ing	⟶	baking
take	+ ing	⟶	taking
come	+ ing	⟶	coming

1. (bake) Maria is _____ rolls today.

2. (come) Tom Butler is _____ in at 9:00 today.

3. (make) Roberto is _____ bread today.

4. (take) Luis is _____ bus #72 to work today.

E. Read the numbers.

30	35	40	45	50	55
thirty	thirty-five	forty	forty-five	fifty	fifty-five

Complete. Use clocks, numbers, and words.

1. _____ 10:40 _____

_____

2. _____

nine-fifty-five

3. _____

_____

4. _____ 1:45 _____

_____

5. _____

twenty-five to six

6. _____

_____

7. _____ _9:30_ _____

8. _____

   ten past three

9. _____

F. Look at the calendar.

AUGUST						
SUNDAY	MONDAY	TUESDAY	WEDNESDAY	THURSDAY	FRIDAY	SATURDAY
			1	2	3	4
5	6	7	8	9	10	11
12	13	14	15	16	17	18
19	20	21	22	23	24	25
26	27	28	29	30	31	

Write the day:

1. August 7   _It's Tuesday._

2. August 17   _____

3. August 27   _____

4. August 11   _____

5. August 1   _____

6. August 26   _____

7. August 23   _____

LESSON 1 At Home

🎧 LISTEN TO THE DIALOG

Maria: When do you get a paycheck?
  Luis: I have my paycheck. Today was payday.
Maria: Good. Why do you look unhappy?
  Luis: They are cheating me.
Maria: What do you mean?
  Luis: I work 80 hours in two weeks. This paycheck is for 40 hours.
Maria: I don't understand. Ask Steve about it.
  Luis: O.K.

📼 COMPREHEND

Listen to the dialog again.
Listen to the questions and respond.

1. Does Luis look happy?

2. Does Luis look happy or unhappy?

3. Are they cheating Luis?

4. When does he get his paycheck?

5. Is it payday?

6. Does Luis have much money?

7. Why does Luis look unhappy?

8. Does Maria understand?

9. Can Steve help Luis?

Listen to the dialog. Check your responses.

PERFORM

Find partners.
Read the dialog aloud with your partners.
Close your books.
Try the dialog again.

PRACTICE

Exercise I

Find a partner. Look at the pictures. Ask "what" questions and respond.
Follow the models.

Model 1: you
Partner 1: What do *you* do every day?
Partner 2: *I* eat apples everyday.

Model 2: Maria

Partner 1: What does *Maria* do every day?
Partner 2: *She* bakes rolls everyday.

a. you and the teacher

b. they

c. Luis and Maria

d. _____

a. the gardener

b. your mother

c. Luis

d. _____

Exercise 2

Find a partner. Look at the pictures. Ask "when" questions about each picture. Respond using the Time Expression List.

Time Expression List

at 11:00   in the morning
at 4:00   in the evening

Model 1: you

Partner 1: When do you paint houses?
Partner 2: I paint houses in the morning.

Model 2: Maria

Partner 1: When does Maria bake rolls?
Partner 2: She bakes rolls in the morning.

---

a. Gloria and Maria
b. you and your teacher
c. they

d. _____

a. Gloria
b. your mother
c. Luis

d. _____

SUMMARY

What do you do every day?	What does Maria do every day?
I bake rolls every day.	She bakes rolls every day.
When do you bake rolls?	When does Maria bake rolls?
I bake rolls in the morning.	She bakes rolls in the morning.

MATCH

Look at the pictures. Read the words. Match the words to the pictures.

_____   _____   _____

1. They are cheating me.

2. I don't understand.

3. Why do you look unhappy?

EXCHANGE

Look at the phrases. Make three conversations with partners. Follow the model.

1. to the movies
   fifteenth (15th)

2. to a soccer game
   fifth (5th)

3. out to dinner
   first (1st) Friday

Partner 1: Do you want to go _to the movies_?
Partner 2: I don't have any money.
Partner 1: When do you get your paycheck?
Partner 2: On the _fifteenth_ of the month.
Partner 1: Well. How about going _to the movies_ then?

At the Personnel Office

TOM BUTLER

🔊 **Listen to the dialog.**

Ann: Hello, Steve. Hello, Luis. Can I help you?

Steve: There is a mistake in Luis' paycheck. He doesn't work 40 hours in two weeks. He works 80.

Ann: Hmm.

Steve: Can we look at his time cards, please?

Ann: Sure.

Luis: Oh no! I don't work from 7:00 to 11:00. I work from 7:00 to 4:00.

Steve: Yes. You punched out at 11:00. You didn't punch in again after lunch.

Ann: Luis, Mr. Butler has to sign this form. Then we can pay you for those 40 hours.

Luis: Thank you, Ann. I understand. I have to punch in twice every day: in the morning and after lunch.

Listen to the dialog again.
Listen to the questions and respond.

1. Is there a mistake in Luis's paycheck?

2. Does he work 40 hours in two weeks?

3. How many hours does he work in two weeks?

4. Does Luis work from 8:00 to 5:00?

5. When does he punch out for lunch?

6. Does Mr. Butler have to sign a form?

7. Can Luis get his money?

8. Does Luis understand?

9. Does he have to punch in twice a day?

10. When does he have to punch in?

Listen to the dialog. Check your responses.

PERFORM

Find partners.
Read the dialog aloud with your partners.
Close your books.
Try the dialog again.

PRACTICE

Exercise

These statements are wrong. Find a partner and correct them. Follow the models.

Model 1: a. Luis works from 7:00 to 11:00.

Partner 1: Luis works from 7:00 to 11:00.
Partner 2: No. He doesn't work from 7:00 to 11:00.

Model 2: b. You wash your car every day.

Partner 1: You wash your car every day.
Partner 2: No. I don't wash my car every day.

---

a. Luis works from 7:00 to 11:00.

b. You wash your car every day.

c. Luis works in a bakery.

d. Robert and Lydia go to school.

e. You and your mother eat lunch at 7:30 in the morning.

f. I teach Chinese.

g. Maria works full-time.

h. Luis works 40 hours in two weeks.

i. You work at Nick's Auto Service.

j. Steve and Bill work at the airport.

k. You and I bake bread every morning.

l. Tom Butler comes in at 11:00.

SUMMARY

I don't work at the airport.

You don't work at the bakery.

He doesn't work at the office.

She doesn't work at Nick's Auto Service.

We don't work at home.

You don't work at school.

They don't work at Nick's Auto Service.

MATCH

Look at the pictures. Read the words. Match the words to the pictures.

_____   _____   _____

1. Oh no!

2. You didn't punch in again after lunch.

3. Can we look at his time cards, please?

INTERACT

Ask partners about name, job, and payday. Make a list.

Examples:

Partner 1: What's your name?
Partner 2: Steve.
Partner 1: What's your job?
Partner 2: Salesman.
Partner 1: When is payday?
Partner 2: The 15th.

NAME	JOB	PAYDAY
Steve	Salesman	15th

▶ EXPRESS AND PRONOUNCE

Listen to these words.
Listen again and repeat.

[*iz*]	[*s*]	[*z*]
washes	plants	goes
teaches	works	sees
changes	cuts	comes
	makes	plays
	eats	repairs
	puts	fills
	looks	claims
		leaves

NOTICE REGISTER

Make four informal and four formal conversations with partners. Follow the models.

Informal
Partner 1: Can I use this *book*?
Partner 2: Sure, go ahead.
Partner 1: Thanks.

  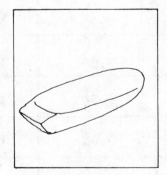 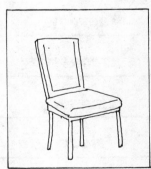

Formal
Partner 1: May I use this *book*?
Partner 2: Certainly.
Partner 1: Thank you.

FIND OUT ABOUT AMERICAN LIFE

I have to punch in twice every day: in the morning and after lunch.

In the United States, many workers use time cards to punch in (start work) and punch out (stop work). Every time they start work or stop work (for example, go to lunch or go home), they put their time cards into a time clock. Then the payroll office looks at the hours on the time cards and writes the paychecks.

Task

Ask three Americans these questions: What's your job?
Do you use a time card?
Then share the responses with the class.

SHOW WHAT YOU KNOW

This is Luis Santos's corrected time card for one week.

Luis Santos	**TIME CARD**			6/15/88
Name				**Period Ending**
	IN	*OUT*	*IN*	*OUT*
Sunday				
Monday	7:00	11:01	12:00	4:05
Tuesday	7:00	11:00	11:58	4:10
Wednesday	7:00	11:05	12:00	4:12
Thursday	7:00	11:00	11:56	4:11
Friday	7:00	11:05	12:00	4:04
Saturday				
			Total Hours	40

Fill in this time card with your work or school hours for the last two weeks.

TIME CARD

Name			Period Ending	
	IN	OUT	IN	OUT
Sunday				
Monday				
Tuesday				
Wednesday				
Thursday				
Friday				
Saturday				
			Total Hours _____	

TEST YOUR KNOWLEDGE

Complete the story. Use the verb list.

Verb List		
can	can't	is
work	works	

Luis doesn't understand his paycheck. He (1) _____ unhappy. Luis (2) _____ 80 hours in two weeks. He doesn't (3) _____ 40 hours. Luis (4) _____ get more money. Mr. Butler has to sign the form. Ann (5) _____ sign the form.

BUILD YOUR SKILLS

A. Complete. Use the words in the list.

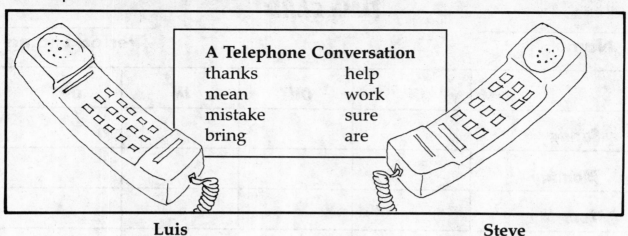

A Telephone Conversation

thanks	help
mean	work
mistake	sure
bring	are

Luis

Steve

L: Hi, Steve! This is Luis.

S: Hi, Luis.

L: Steve, they _____ cheating me.

S: Hun?

L: There's a _____ in my paycheck.

S: What do you _____?

L: The paycheck is for 40 hours. But I _____ 80.

S: Hmm.

L: Can you _____ me?

S: Yeah. _____ your check to work tomorrow.

L: _____ a lot, Steve.

S: _____. Bye.

L: Bye.

This is Luis' paycheck for 40 hours. It is not correct.

Nick's Auto Service
Seattle, Washington

June 22, 1988

Pay to the Order of _____ **Luis Santos** _____ | 142.00 |

One hundred forty-two ------------------------------- **no/100**   *Dollars*

First Interstate of Washington

Nick Godis

B. Nick Gadis gives Luis a new check for 80 hours. The check is for $284.00. Complete the check.

Nick's Auto Service
Seattle, Washington

_____

Pay to the
Order of _____   [   ]

_____ Dollars

**First Interstate
of Washington**

_____

C. Read the response. Write a question.

1. _____ Yes, you can.

2. _____ In the morning.

3. _____ She bakes rolls.

4. _____ No, they don't.

5. _____ In the kitchen.

6. _____ Yes, he does.

7. _____ On the 15th of the month.

8. _____ I teach English.

D. Look at the pictures. Make statements.

Marie works in the bakery. Luis doesn't.

1. work in the bakery

_____

2. work full-time

_____

3. bake bread every morning

_____

4. come at 9:00

_____

5. repair cars

_____

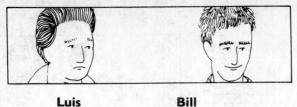

Luis   Bill

6. wash cars

_____

E. Spelling: -s

bake + s ⟶	bakes	Maria *bakes* pies.
bring + s ⟶	brings	
help + s ⟶	helps	
make + s ⟶	makes	
repair + s ⟶	repairs	
work + s ⟶	works	

Complete. Use the words in the list.

bake	help
bring	repair
do	make
work	

Maria and Luis have jobs. Maria _____ in a bakery. She _____ bread, rolls, and pies. Luis _____ not. He _____ cars at Nick's Auto Service. He _____ home a paycheck two times a month. At night, Luis _____ the children with their homework, and Maria _____ dinner.

F. Look at the pictures. Write a story.

Luis eats breakfast at 6:00 every morning. _____

_____

_____

_____

_____

_____

G. Numbers

60	70	80	90	100
sixty	seventy	eighty	ninety	one hundred

1¢ penny   5¢ nickel   10¢ dime   25¢ quarter   50¢ half dollar

Count the Money.

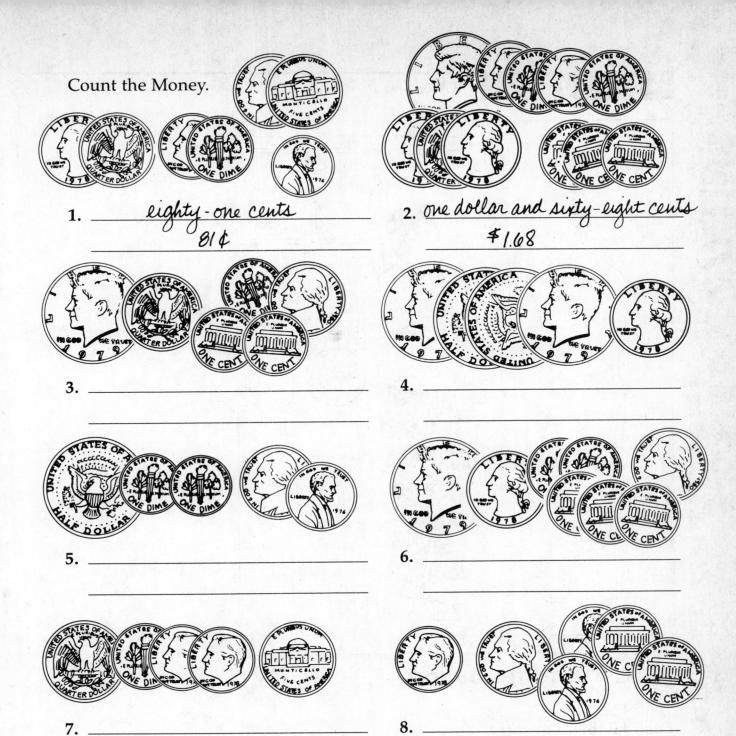

1. _eighty-one cents_
   81¢

2. _one dollar and sixty-eight cents_
   $1.68

3. _____

4. _____

5. _____

6. _____

7. _____

8. _____

LESSON 1 At Work

🔊 LISTEN TO THE DIALOG

Bill: Hi, Luis.
Luis: Hi, Bill. I'm sorry . . .
Bill: Yeah. You usually get here on time.
Luis: Yeah. I am punching in late today. The bus . . .
Bill: Oh. All the buses are running on new schedules.
Luis: New schedules? Why?
Bill: School starts this week. Bus schedules always change then. There are some new schedules in the office.
Luis: Good.
Bill: Let's get one at lunch time.
Luis: O.K.

⊙ COMPREHEND

Listen to the dialog again.
Listen to the questions and respond.

1. Is Luis late?
2. Why is Luis sorry?
3. Does Luis usually get to work on time?
4. Are the buses running on new schedules?
5. Do the bus schedules change this week?
6. Does school start this week?
7. When does school start?
8. Can Luis get a new bus schedule?
9. When can Luis get a new schedule?

Listen to the dialog. Check your responses.

PERFORM

Find partners.
Read the dialog aloud with your partners.
Close your books.
Try the dialog again.

PRACTICE

Exercise 1

Find a partner. Make sentences. Follow the models.

> **Model:** a. Roberto and Lydia   eat lunch at 12:00
>   eat lunch at 11:00
>
> **Partner 1: Roberto and Lydia usually eat** lunch at 12:00.
> **Partner 2: Today they are eating** at 11:00.

> **Model:** b. Luis   punch in on time   punch in late
>
> **Partner 1: Luis usually punches in** on time.
> **Partner 2: Today he is punching in** late.

Name	Usually	Today
a. Roberto and Lydia	eat lunch at 12:00	eat lunch at 11:00
b. Luis	punch in on time	punch in late
c. Ernesto and Gloria	take the bus to school	take a taxi to school
d. I	go to school by bus	go to school by car
e. Maria	go to the bakery	go to the airport
f. Robert	bake bread	bake rolls
g. You	teach in Room 110	teach in Room 105
h. Steve	work in the sales dept.	work in the service dept.

Exercise 2

Find a partner. Use the information in the chart. Ask questions and respond. Follow the models.

> **Model 1:** a. Roberto and Lydia   eat lunch at 12:00
>   eat lunch at 11:00
>
> **Partner 1: Do Roberto and Lydia usually eat** lunch at 12:00?
> **Partner 2:** Yes, but **today they're eating** at 11:00.

| Model 2: | b. Luis | punch in on time | punch in late |

Partner 1: Does Luis usually punch in on time?
Partner 2: Yes, but **today he is punching in** late.

SUMMARY

Roberto and Lydia usually eat lunch at 12:00.
Today they are eating at 11:00.

Does Luis usually punch in on time?
Yes, but **today he is punching in** late.

MATCH

Look at the pictures. Read the words. Match the words to the pictures.

_____ _____ _____

1. New schedules? Why?

2. I'm sorry.

3. You usually get here on time.

EXCHANGE

Look at the pictures. Make three conversations. Follow the model.

1. go to school
   work

2. bake apple pies
   cook chicken

3. work in the bakery
   look for an
   apartment

Partner 1: Does your mother usually

___*go to school*___?

Partner 2: Yeah, she does, but she isn't

___*going to school*___ today.

Partner 1: Why not?

Partner 2: She's ___*working*___.

LESSON 2 In Mr. Butler's Office

🔊 LISTEN TO THE DIALOG

Luis: I'm sorry I'm late, Mr. Butler.
Tom: You are usually on time, Luis. This is your first late day.
Luis: Today is Monday, too!
Tom: Yes. Please call us the next time. We always have some early customers on Monday.
Luis: O.K.
Tom: Can you stay after 4:00 today?
Luis: After 4:00?
Tom: There's a lot of work to do.
Luis: O.K.

🔊 COMPREHENSION

Listen to the dialog again.
Listen to the questions and respond.

1. Is Luis usually late?

2. Is Luis late today?

3. Is today Monday?

4. Is this Luis's first late day?

5. What day is today?

6. Do customers come in early on Monday?

7. Can Luis stay after 4:00 today?

8. Is there a lot of work?

Listen to the dialog. Check your responses.

PERFORM

Find partners.
Read the dialog aloud with your partners.
Close your books.
Try the dialog again.

PRACTICE

Exercise I

Find a partner. Ask questions and respond. Follow the models.

> **Model 1:** a. Maria and Luis   work to do
>
> **Partner 1:** Are **Maria and Luis** busy tonight?
> **Partner 2:** Yes, **they have** a lot of **work to do**.

> **Model 2:** b. Maria   gardening to do
>
> **Partner 1:** Is **Maria** busy today?
> **Partner 2:** Yes, **she has** a lot of **gardening to do**.

a. Maria and Luis   work to do

b. Maria   gardening to do

c. the children   homework to do

d. you   houses to paint

e. Luis   tools to put away

f. your sister   lunches to make

g. you and your brother cars to wash

h. Lydia   flowers to plant

Exercise 2

Find a partner. Ask questions and respond "no." Follow the models.

> **Model 1:** a. Maria and Luis   work to do
>
> **Partner 1:** Do **Maria and Luis have** a lot of **work to do** on
> Mondays?
> **Partner 2:** No, **they don't**.

> **Model 2:** b. Maria   gardening to do
>
> **Partner 1:** Does **Maria have** a lot of **gardening to do** on
> weekends?
> **Partner 2:** No, **she doesn't**.

SUMMARY

Are **Maria and Luis** busy tonight?	Yes, **they have** a lot of **work to do**.
Is **Maria** busy tonight?	Yes, she has a lot of gardening to do.
Do you have a lot of **houses to paint**?	**No, I don't.**
Does Luis have a lot of **tools to put away**?	**No, he doesn't.**

MATCH

Look at the pictures. Read the words. Match the words to the pictures.

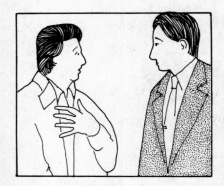  

_____   _____   _____

1. After 4:00?
2. I'm sorry I'm late.
3. Please call us the next time.

INTERACT

Find a partner. Make a conversation for each situation. Perform for the class.

Partner 1: You come late for work. You missed the bus. Say you are sorry.
Partner 2: Tell Partner 1 what he should do.

Partner 1: You are late for class. Tell your teacher why.
Partner 2: Accept the apology.

EXPRESS AND PRONOUNCE

Listen to the -s at the end of the words in these expressions. Pronounce the -s at the beginning of the next word. Draw a circle around the -s and the next word. Follow the model.

The schedule(s are) new today.

New routes often run late.

We have customers on Monday.

There's a lot of work to do.

Do all workers at the office lose money?

NOTICE REGISTER

Informal
Make three informal conversations with partners. Follow the model.

Partner 1: Why are you *doing your homework* late? You usually do it on time.
Partner 2: I'm sorry. My bus was late.

1. do your homework
2. wash the cars
3. make dinner

Formal
Make three formal conversations with partners. Follow the model.

Partner 1: I'm sorry that I'm late.
Partner 2: You usually *come to work* on time. Next time please call.
Partner 1: I will.

1. come to work
2. come to the office
3. punch in

FIND OUT ABOUT AMERICAN LIFE

Please call us the next time.

In the U.S., it is important to be on time. Call if:
1. You will be late.
2. You can not come.

Task

Who do you call if you are going to be late for school?
What is the telephone number?

SHOW WHAT YOU KNOW

Look at the bus schedule. Answer the questions.

3rd	Denny Way	NE 45th	NE 55th
6:15	6:21	6:34	6:41
6:45	6:51	7:05	7:12
7:15	7:21	7:36	7:43
7:45	7:51	8:05	8:12
8:15	8:21	8:36	8:43

Luis takes the bus to Nick's Auto Service. Work starts at 7:00. He gets off the bus on NE 55th near Nick's Auto Service. He gets on the bus at 3rd Avenue. Maria takes the bus to the bakery. Her work starts at 8:45. She gets on the bus on Denny Way. She gets off the bus at NE 45th.

1. When does Luis take the bus? _____

2. What time does he get off the bus? _____

3. What time does Maria take the bus? _____

4. What time does she get off the bus? _____

TEST YOUR KNOWLEDGE

Complete the sentences. Use the list. Follow the model.

can't	can	first	last
come	leave	on time	late
doesn't have	has	left	right
don't have	have	that	this

1. I can't play soccer, but I _____can_____ play basketball.

2. Go left at the corner, not _____.

3. Use this chair, not _____ chair.

4. Santos is not her _____ name. It's her

   _____ name.

5. I _____ a job, my wife has a job.

6. I come to work at 8:00 and I _____ at 5:00.

7. My brother doesn't have a daughter. He _____
   a son.

8. He's always _____ on weekends, but he's on
   time on weekdays.

BUILD YOUR SKILLS

A. Complete. Use the words in the list.

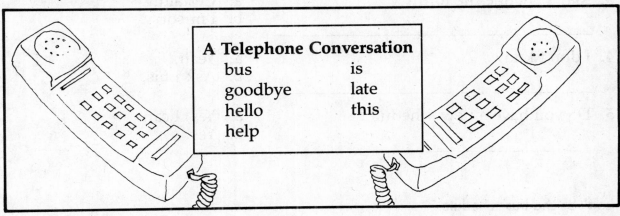

A Telephone Conversation

bus	is
goodbye	late
hello	this
help	

Partner 1: Hello, _____ Tom there?

Partner 2: Just a minute please.

Partner 3: _____. This is Tom. Can I _____ you?

Partner 1: Tom. _____ is Luis Santos. I missed my

   _____. I will be 30 minutes _____.

Partner 3: Thanks for calling, Luis.

Partner 1: O.K. _____.

B. Complete.

	Full Form	Contraction		Full Form	Contraction
1.	_____	don't	6.	_____	aren't
2.	_____	isn't	7.	do not	_____
3.	does not	_____	8.	_____	I'm not
4.	are not	_____	9.	_____	doesn't
5.	I am not	_____	10.	is not	_____

C. Read. Respond with *a* or *b*. Write the response.

1. Can you stay after 4:00 today?

   _____

   a. Yes, it is.
   b. After 4:00?

2. I'm sorry that I'm late.

   _____

   a. Please call the next time.
   b. Yeah. Good luck.

3. May I change the form?

   _____

   a. Certainly.
   b. I'm sorry.

4. I don't know.

   _____

   a. Yeah.
   b. Ask Luis.

5. Do you have a new schedule?

   _____

   a. Yes, I can.
   b. Yes.

Look at the bus schedule.

NE 55th	NE 45th	Denny Way	3rd Ave
3:50	3:57	4:10	4:16
4:20	4:27	4:40	4:46
4:50	4:57	5:12	5:18
5:20	5:27	5:41	5:47

D. Read. Write the response.

1. What time does the 3:50 bus get to Denny Way? _____

2. When does the 4:20 bus get to NE 45th? _____

3. Maria takes the 4:57 bus from NE 45th. What time does she get to 3rd Avenue? _____

4. Luis takes the 5:20 bus from NE 55th. When does he get to 3rd Avenue? _____

E. Spelling: -es

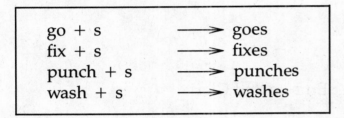

```
go  + s      ------>  goes
fix + s      ------>  fixes
punch + s    ------>  punches
wash + s     ------>  washes
```

Complete. Use the words in the list.

Luis _____ to work every morning. He _____ in at
    go   punch

7:00. Luis usually _____ cars, and he sometimes
         fix

_____ cars. Luis _____ home at 4:15.
 wash   go

F. Complete the crossword. Use the words in the list.

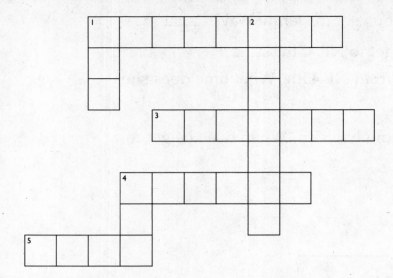

bakery
bus
can
children
eats
repairs
usually

Across

1. Luis and Maria have two _____, Ernesto and Gloria.

3. Luis _____ gets to work on time.

4. Maria works in a _____.

5. Luis _____ lunch at 11:00.

Down

1. Maria _____ bake bread.

2. Luis _____ cars at Nick's Auto Service.

4. The children take the _____ to school.

G. What time is it?

seven o'clock   It's 7:00.

seven fifteen;   It's 7:15.
quarter after seven

seven thirty;   It's 7:30.
half past seven

seven forty-five;   It's 7:45.
quarter to eight

Complete. Use clocks, numbers, and words.

1. _____ It's 6:30.

2. _____ It's _____.

3. _____ It's 8:15.

4. _____ It's _____.

5. nine forty-five   It's _____.

6. two thirty   It's _____.